What animals live here?

DESERTS

Mary-Jane Wilkins

W

FRANKLIN WATTS
LONDON·SYDNEY

Franklin Watts
First published in Great Britain in 2016 by
The Watts Publishing Group

For Brown Bear Books Ltd:
Picture Researcher: Clare Newman
Designer: Melissa Roskell
Design Manager: Keith Davis
Editorial Director: Lindsey Lowe
Children's Publisher: Anne O'Daly

ISBN 978 1 4451 5172 4

Printed in China

Franklin Watts
An imprint of
Hachette Children's Group
Part of The Watts Publishing Group
Carmelite House
50 Victoria Embankment
London EC4Y 0DZ

An Hachette UK company
www.hachette.co.uk

www.franklinwatts.co.uk

CONTENTS

Where are the DESERTS?

There are deserts all around the world. There are hot deserts and cold deserts. They are all very dry places.

The **biggest** desert is Antarctica. In this cold desert rain falls as snow. Less than 5 cm falls every year.

Sahara

Antarctica

WOW!

The **biggest** hot desert
is the Sahara in North Africa.
This has just under 2.5 cm
of rain every year.

Animals in deserts have very little
water to drink. The biggest desert
animals are camels. They can
go without water for a long time.
You can find out about them
and other desert animals in this book.

CAMELS

Most camels are dromedaries. They have one hump on their back and live in Africa and the Middle East.

Another type of camel has two humps. These are called Bactrian camels. They live in Asia.

Camels have two rows of long eyelashes to keep sand out of their eyes. They can close their nostrils in a sandstorm.

Camels have very **wide** feet so they can walk over sand without sinking.

MEERKAT

Meerkats are the same size as squirrels. They live in **big** groups in Southern Africa.

Meerkats eat insects, lizards, eggs and fruit.

Sometimes meerkats stand on their back legs. They look out for predators that might eat them. A hawk or eagle could fly down and **snatch** them.

When a meerkat sees a bird, it gives a warning cry. All the meerkats scurry to their burrows.

CARACAL

This wild cat can go for a long time without a drink. It rests during the hottest part of the day. In the early morning or cool evening it hunts birds and small animals.

Big ears help a caracal hear very well.

These cats are amazing **jumpers**.
They can knock a bird out
of the air 3 m above them.
They run *very fast* and can
catch prey three times their size.

ARMADILLO LIZARD

The armadillo lizard lives in the desert in Southern Africa. It has **tough**, brownish outer skin. This helps it hide in the desert sand. This lizard eats termites and other insects as well as plants.

If an animal attacks, the lizard rolls into a ball. Only the tough outer skin shows.

The thorny devil has scaly skin and sharp **spikes**. They stop animals eating it.

THORNY DEVIL

This small lizard lives in Australia. It walks under wet plants so water drips on its scales. The water runs down the lizard's body and into its mouth.

FENNEC FOX

The fennec fox is small, but it has **huge** ears. It is only 20 cm tall, but its ears can be as much as 15 cm long. Big ears mean that the fox can hear very well.

The fennec fox's big ears help to keep it cool.

Fennec foxes hunt at night when it is cool. They eat beetles and other insects, lizards and birds.

SIDEWINDER

This snake moves sideways over hot sand. Only two small parts of its scaly body touch the sand as it moves. This stops the snake getting too hot.

Sidewinders are the same colour as the sand they hide in.

Sidewinders are predators. They eat lizards and birds. They lie in wait for their prey. The snake buries its body under the sand. Just its head shows. If a lizard comes near, it **grabs** and swallows it.

JERBOA

This tiny mouse has very **l o n g** back legs. These help it to hop, just like a kangaroo.

WOW!

This little mouse may never drink. It gets all the water it needs from the food it eats.

A jerboa can **jump** 3 m when it is trying to get away from a snake or bird that wants to eat it.

TERMITES

These insects build **giant** mounds. Under each mound is a nest. Here the queen termite lays her eggs. Termites eat dead plants and wood. Lizards, snakes and birds eat termites.

WOW!

Termite nests can hold 20 million insects. The queen is the biggest. She can be 10 cm long.

Termites build their mounds from dried mud. The mounds can be 7.6 m high.

DESERT FACTS

Hot deserts are dry, but not hot all the time. At night the temperature can drop to 0°Celsius.

The hottest place in North America is called Death Valley. It is in the Mojave Desert in California. Here it can be 57°Celsius in the summer. →

The driest place on Earth is the Atacama Desert. It is in South America. No rain fell on parts of the Atacama Desert for 420 years.

USEFUL WORDS

burrow

An underground home dug by an animal.

predator

An animal that hunts and →
kills other animals for food.
The sidewinder is a predator.

prey

An animal hunted and eaten
by another animal. Lizards
are the prey of a sidewinder.

scales

The tough layer on the outside of a lizard
or snake. Scales protect the animal.

FIND OUT MORE

Discover Science: Desert,
Nicola Davies, Kingfisher, 2012.

Exploring Deserts,
Anita Ganeri, Raintree, 2015.

Life Cycles: Desert, Sean Callery,
Kingfisher, 2013.

Saving Wildlife: Desert Animals,
Sonya Newland, Franklin Watts,
2014.

INDEX